Cla...
V...

CW00726468

FORTY YEARS
OF THE
FORD TRANSIT
1965-2005

Robert Berry

Nostalgia Road Publications

CONTENTS

The **Nostalgia Road** Series ™

is produced under licence by

Nostalgia Road Publications Ltd.

Units 5 - 8, Chancel Place, Shap Road Industrial Estate,

Kendal, Cumbria, LA9 6NZ

Tel. +44 (0)1539 738832 - Fax: +44 (0)1539 730075

designed and published by

Trans-Pennine Publishing Ltd.

PO Box 10, Appleby-in-Westmorland, Cumbria, CA16 6FA

Tel. +44 (0)17683 51053 Fax. +44 (0)17683 53558

e-mail: admin@transpenninepublishing.co.uk

and printed by

Kent Valley Colour Printers Ltd.

Kendal, Cumbria - +44 (0)1539 741344

Front Cover: *In the summer of 2005, the Ford Motor Company celebrated 40 years of continual production on their Transit models. Although the range was really extensive our cover photograph provides comparisons of the evolution of the vans during the past four decades. The oldest MkI model is on the left, and the newest incarnation is seen on the right.*

Rear Cover Top: *This image of an early Ford Transit van portrays it fullfilling the roll they were intended for, that of light delivery and collection work.*

Rear Cover Bottom: *Celebrating the birth of the Transit, several generations of the Transit are seen during the road run from Essex to the Transit plant at Southampton, which was staged to mark the 40th anniversary of the Transit. In the lead is the 1965 GEC-Elliott Automation MkI Transit that was restored by Ford.*

Title Page: *The showpiece of Ford's commercial vehicle activities was the Southampton plant. The factory covered 1.5m sq. ft and had the most modern commercial vehicle assembly line in Europe. When the Production Building opened in 1973, it was producing 260 Transits per day, making it Europe's most successful commercial vehicle in 1973.*

ISBN 1 903016 61 4

British Cataloguing in Publication Data

A catalogue record for this book is available from the British Library

INTRODUCTION

There can be no doubt, that the Ford Transit range of light commercial vehicles has become a living legend, and after four decades of continuous production few can deny that this truly is 'The Van of the Century'! Over the years much has been written about the Transit, but the subject still holds much fascination. As a result, and with the kind co-operation of the manufacturers, this short overview of the model range has been produced to mark those 40 glorious years. This project began as a result of a conversation almost a decade ago between Simon Sproule of Ford's Corporate Affairs and my series editor, just after the Transit had enjoyed its 30th Anniversary, following which I was ultimately given the task of producing this account.

Above: *Our picture here gives a very accurate comparison of the Transit family, with MkIII, MkII and MkI models running from left to right.*

Of course the Transit did not just evolve overnight, for Ford of Great Britain have been adapting or specially producing commercial vehicles almost as long as the company has been manufacturing cars. The narrative therefore goes back into the history of the company, starting with what was probably their most famous product, the Model T, and brings it right up to date in 2005. A century of commercial vehicle history follows, with the Ford Transit claiming a massive 40% share in it.

Robert Berry **Penrith 2006**

3

FORD LIGHT COMMERCIALS BEFORE THE TRANSIT

The very first products that Ford imported into this country from America as far back as 1904, were the Model A two-cylinder, 8hp cars. It was an adaptation of one of the first dozen of these cars that can be considered as the first British Ford commercial vehicle manufactured.

However, it was the Model T that would become one of the greatest selling vehicles of all time, and as a commercial vehicle it was supplied in both standard and long-wheelbase options. Ford very quickly established an enviable reputation as a maker of light commercial vehicles and from 1917 onwards, the company built the TT Model for a greater payload. As can be imagined from the model code, this could accommodate a greater capacity on its longer (124") wheelbase, and was available as a van, a truck and even a bus.

Above: *Following the trucks based on the Model T car, Ford later designed specific commercial vehicles. Pictured here is the very last vehicle coming off the production line at Trafford Park, Manchester, a Model A van.*

When the Model T was replaced by a new Model A, it was also offered as a van or pick-up truck from the end of 1927. Two commercial versions, the 10-cwt Model A and the 30-cwt Model AA, which was built on a wheelbase of 132", some 29" longer than the smaller model. Both versions were powered by a 24hp four-cylinder engine, but the smaller model also had the option of having a 14hp engine fitted for economy. It was actually a 10-cwt Model A van that is credited with being the last vehicle off the production line from Ford's original British factory at Trafford Park, Manchester in 1931. Following this, Ford moved their manufacturing operation to Dagenham, in Essex.

The successors to the Model A commercials were introduced in 1932, these being built at Dagenham. Once again two variants were offered, these being the Model B and the Model BB. With the introduction of these, Ford acquired an improved image. The radiator core of these new models was now behind a radiator shell which protected the core and made cleaning the vehicle a much easier process. Within two years of the introduction of these B and BB ranges, Ford offered the BBE model, which was a forward-control version for customers who required a greater load area from the same class of vehicle. This vehicle retailed at a commendable £286. An option for these vehicles was the fitting of a V8 engine, and these proved so extremely popular that within a very short time this became the standard power plant for the range.

As the Depression of the early-1930s eased, large American-inspired, car-derived vans powered by V8 engines became extremely popular with many businesses. Ford made the most on this, and a rather bewildering array of model codes succeeded, or complimented one another.

Yet, for the more economy-minded small business user, Ford had also introduced their Y models. These commercial vehicles were based on the 8hp, four-cylinder, side-valve saloon cars that were put into production during August 1932, an incredibly brief 10 months after design work had begun.

Above: *This example of a Ford Model A has survived into preservation against all odds, especially given the hard-working lives of most light commercials.*

Above *During the Depression of the 1930s there was a major 'fall off' in demand for motor vehicles, especially those of American origin. Yet, as the 1930s progressed, lightweight, car-derived vans again became popular and a market for larger light commercials re-emerged, these tended to be American inspired vehicles as this 15-cwt Ford E98C model.*

However during April 1938, Ford introduced an entirely new model, specifically for the British market in the 10-cwt class, this being the Fordson E83W range. These semi-forward control vehicles were powered by a 10hp side-valve, four-cylinder 1172cc engine, and built on a 7' 6" wheelbase. But as the driving position had been moved forward, which was achieved by having an offset engine, a load space of 6' 8" was possible.

These models were available as a van, a pick-up truck or chassis cab for the specialist body-building trade. Soon a great number of these models were to be seen in Britain as auxiliary kitchens during the period of World War II. Although the E83W range of commercials were to prove practical and reliable machines, very little further development was implemented during the rather long life of these models.

The trailing edge of the rear wings was altered in shape during 1946, and twin rear lights were fitted on the panel below the rear doors from September 1954. Yet, with all the technical advancement taking place by other manufactures during the 1950s, coupled to customer requirements for greater cab comfort after the long years of 'make do and mend,' this was really a very poor response to market demands.

Ford were therefore fighting a losing battle. During the mid-1950s, they were still pitching their rather old fashioned, composite (steel panelling over a wooden frame) constructed, E83W commercial range in a very highly competitive market. Their consistently close rival, Bedford (which was the commercial arm of the Vauxhall motor company), were now beginning to dominate this market with their own highly successful range of CA models.

The Fordson E83W was by no means an inferior vehicle, but this model had been introduced as far back as 1938, and obviously within the 19 years that these models were produced, a great deal of new development had been achieved by motor manufacturers. Expecting a 15-year-old design to compete in a market that offered customers not only the up-to-date Bedford CA, but also new models from Austin, Morris, Standard and Commer was crazy. The competition unfortunately emphasised how antiquated the E83W, with its high and narrow styling and separate wings, had become. So for all the versatility and reliability that the E83W offered, it was never the less on an uphill climb to compete with its peers.

In an effort to win back a healthy portion of a lucrative market, in which the E83W had been the leader in its time, Ford introduced their new 400E range of models on 1st November 1957. This was a completely new design and built as a fully forward-control vehicle with a tried and tested 1700 cc four-cylinder engine mounted in the cab between the two seats. Day-to-day service on this power unit being carried out by the simple task of raising a forward-hinged cover inside the cab.

Top Right: *An excellent candidate for an enthusiast to devote love and affection on, to say nothing of hard work. Here we see one of the truck variants of the E83W.*

Middle Right: *A period publicity picture of an E494C van, although it shows how good the vehicle was for sign-writing, the base colour of 'Barbie' pink must have been an eye-opener back when car colours were more staid. Note will be made in this view of the radiator grille, which of course differed on these five-cwt vans.*

Bottom Right: *The E83W models had quite a long production life, as they were introduced before World War II and remained virtually unchanged until 1957. This rear view of a Rochdale-registered van was photographed in Halifax during the late-1970s. As can be seen by the styling line on the rear wings, this is a late model.* Author's collection

The new Ford 400E models had a greater carrying capacity, offered as either 10/12-cwt or 15-cwt models and they came in various formats, including a van, a pick-up truck and a minibus. Chassis-cowl and chassis-cab versions were also marketed, and this offered scope for enterprising builders to create special body applications on the new chassis,

In retrospect, these Ford 400E models had the disadvantage that the cab could only accommodate two people, as the engine was badly positioned between the two front seats. This meant that models were not practical for serving in roles where the driver had access to the load area from the cab. Also with the engine being situated within the cab, it tended to provide a rather noisy environment for the driver and his passenger.

On the other hand the model had maximised load space, and whilst being of forward-control layout it was extremely practical for manoeuvring around crowded city streets. The 400E had the advantage of a tried and trusted power unit that was then being produced for the popular Ford Consul. As this was in production from 1956 to 1962, reconditioned units and spares were no problem for future commercial vehicle owners.

The styling of the 400E range was very up-to-date, especially when compared to the obviously dated look of the E83W. With side windows, various mini-bus seating arrangements could be chosen and they could also be built into ambulances or even very attractive motor-caravans. Indeed, with only minor conversions, enterprising companies could produce an entirely different kind of application to the basic form.

Top Left: *This photograph was taken at the Barnard Castle truck show during 2005. This is one of the relatively few examples of the Ford 400E model 15-cwt trucks that are now preserved for future posterity.*

Middle Left: *Comparable to the 400E was the German-built Ford Taunus, which also served similar market need. This rear view of an hotel bus, illustrates a commendable luggage space and ample passenger room.*

Bottom Left: *As well as the truck, van, mini-bus and chassis-cab/cowl versions, the motor-home was a popular variant. Although normally produced by specialist convertors, some people converted basic models into caravans by adding rear windows and paying the relevant tax on doing so. This example was photographed at Grange Moor, between Huddersfield and Wakefield several years ago; note the positioning of the spare wheel.* Author's collection

Yet despite Ford's best efforts, the Bedford CA range reigned supreme in this market. Curiously in the lighter 5/7-cwt market, Ford suffered the same problems, this time against the Morris 1000. For although the 300E vans based on the Anglia and Prefect 100E - three-speed gearbox models, and the later 307E vans, were extremely good vehicles, they could never seem to break the monopoly that the British Motor Corporation had. It was not really until British Leyland (the successors of BMC) replaced the Minor with the troubled Marina, that Ford finally started to become the market leader in this sector with their range of Escort vans (introduced in the late 1960s),

Even so, it should come as no surprise that a company with such a long history of producing just exactly what the customer wants, should eventually come up with a winner in both the 5/7-cwt and 10/15-cwt markets, the latter of course being conquered by the Transit, which was launched in 1965.

Above: *Ford of Great Britain produced the Thames 400E range in various formats, including basic van, (shown here), truck, pick-up, minibus, or chassis-cab/cowl options for specialist body builders.*

The foundations for the new 10- to 15-cwt range were, like so many other durable and well respected designs, based on a history of gradual and consistent evolution, by acting on continual reliability tests and listening to customer feedback. The relatively disappointing sales performance of the 400E had, by 1960, set management at Ford scratching their heads about the way forward, certainly from the mid-1960s, when the 400E would have to be replaced. As the world's premier car and commercial vehicle manufacturing organisation, Ford could not countenance a situation where its products were lagging well behind the competition.

THE PAN-EUROPEAN VAN PROJECT

The way forward had to be with some radical thinking, in both the 5/7-cwt and the 10/15cwt ranges, and whilst the adoption of American-influenced styling and engineering were profoundly experienced in Ford's car ranges, the company felt a certain passive resistance to this approach in the light commercial vehicle sector. The American panel van may have been what Europeans needed at the time, but you would have had a hard job convincing anyone that this was the case.

The seeds for any new model's success would have to be sown in ground that had been thoroughly cultivated well in advance. Therefore the concept for a Pan-European delivery van was thoroughly researched, as were the models produced by the competition. Ford's own products did not escape detailed scrutiny, neither did the firm's manufacturing plants.

Above: *Although very much in keeping with its peers, with its stylish sculptured front and forward-control layout, the 400E models did not reach the sales target that the management had hoped for. Yet with its short wheel-base resulting in ease of manoeuvring and the useful side-loading door, they were ideal vehicles for congested city streets.*

The main object of attention was the runaway success of Ford's main rival Vauxhall Motors, who were owned by the American firm, General Motors. They produced the very modern and versatile Bedford CA range of vehicles, which had been introduced in 1952 and massively revised in 1959. To compete against these, as well as the products from other British manufacturers (such as BMC and the Rootes Group), Ford had to be very careful in their next offering, as there was little room for another commercial failure.

A major element in the success of the CA was its wide availability as either a chassis-cab or a chassis-cowl, which were then used by specialist bodybuilders for minibus, ambulance, motor-caravan, mobile-shop, milk float and ice-cream van applications. Few of these builders liked the 400E, for the reason that 1703cc power unit was situated between the seats, which rather had the disadvantage that the cab could only accommodate two people and be rather noisy too. After listening to customer feedback, Ford of Great Britain soon recognised that this was a serious problem, yet although a completely new model was needed, they could not finance such a project in their own right.

At this same time the Ford factory in Germany was also producing their Taunus van, which was very much along similar styling lines to the 400E. Although excellent vehicles in their own right, it too was not enjoying the success that Ford had hoped for in this market.

In the early-1960s, each plant kept its own identity, but someone in Ford's corporate headquarters in the USA began to wonder, whether or not they might 'kill two lame ducks with one stone.' So after much debate, it was decided to unite the resources of both operations, and produce a new medium weight commercial vehicle that would be capable of being built in either factory, which could then be marketed throughout Europe. Accordingly, the Pan European Van project was first muted in 1961, and each of the two partner plants were asked to draw up what they felt to be the most important criteria that the yet-to-be-appointed design team would have to consider.

Below: *This illustration of the German Ford Taunus shows the similarity between the British Ford 400E model . Both models shared a forward-control layout, plus similar styling features and dimensions. These models were in production prior to the introduction of the now world famous Ford Transit.*

The Birth Of A Legend, The MkI Transit

To the team who were responsible for the design of the new 'Van for Europe' project, it was essential to gather as much data as possible to ascertain the merits of the competition. Also the principle failures of the Ford Thames 400E models made in Britain, and the Ford Taunus FK built in Cologne (Koln) models. Both of these were styled along the same principle concept, a boxy forward-control vehicle with a nicely rounded cab. This arrangement rather echoed American practice at this time, but the ideas were employed on a smaller scale and a reasonable 10- to 15-cwt payload capacity. The question was whether the Pan-European Van Project should go forward from the existing product range, or go back to the drawing-board completely.

Above: *Little did Ford realise in 1965, but they were about to unleash an iconoclast upon the transport world. Illustrated here is a variant in the enormous Ford Transit range. The photograph clearly shows the substantial body of this drop-side truck in the bright livery of the well known fleet of the civil engineering company Wimpey.*

An American, by the name of Ed Baumgartner who was a product planner for Ford, was appointed the leader of the design team which was assembled in Britain during 1961. The team were based in what was, at the time, part of the then Ford of Britain parts warehouse at South Ockenden in Essex. Their brief simply called for a vehicle that encompassed the 12- to 30-cwt commercial vehicle range, that would be robust, comfortable, economical in operation and cheap and easy to maintain.

From the outset, the design team considered it prudent to consult both Ford's sales agents and industrial/commercial users as to what they thought to be an ideal type of vehicle. They also held lengthy discussions with drivers of all kinds, but they were particularly interested in the views of ambulance and other emergency service crews. This was considered crucial to ascertain what was actually an ideal vehicle from the drivers point of view.

As it would be the drivers of the vehicles who would be more closely involved with the day to day running of the vehicles than anyone else, it was logical to listen to their views. It was also part of a clever marketing exercise, as it was hoped that the new Pan-European van would lead the way in the rather lucrative ambulance, fire and police vehicle market. This obviously had the possibility of a knock-on effect, for as Volkswagen had found with their Transporter model, sales in this discriminating market sector could automatically promote further sales in the slightly less discriminating markets of trade and industry.

A further consideration was the area of mini- and crew-bus operations, where the 400E and Taunus had done rather well. This was a potentially huge market, and it was again an area where the Transporter in its Kombi and Micro-bus form was doing particularly well all over Europe.

Top Right: *The entirely new Ford Transit propelled light commercial vehicles into a new era and they instantly took the lion's share of the market. They also proved that a commercial vehicle could be stylish and comfortable as well as practical.*

Middle Right: *This 1967 diesel drop-side truck is painted in the livery of Moss Bay Metals of Workington, on the Cumbrian coast. This is an excellent example of one of the few early Transits that have been preserved. Seen here attending the Heart of the Lakes Vintage Vehicle Rally in Penrith, which was organised by the publishers of this book to help the area after the tragedy of the foot and mouth epidemic in 2001.*
Trans-Pennine Publishing Archive

Bottom Right: *At first glance this looks like the typical diesel engine Transit van, but RKK 278G, is actually one of the comparatively rare 4WD models dating from 1968. These variants proved very popular as they enabled surveyors and civil engineers to perform their duties. Yet there were also examples in the emergency service fleets, particularly the fire service, and in utility undertakings like the regional electricity boards who used them in power line maintenance work.*

Above: *The first British Transit came off the production lines at the Langley factory in Berkshire on 9th August 1965. During 1972, Transit Production began at Ford's Southampton plant, which is illustrated in our very impressive aerial view.*

Baumgartner and his design team were in the enviable position that they were virtually given a clean sheet of paper for the new project. Yet, to keep the new model as cost-effective as possible, many of the components to be used (particularly the more expensive ones to develop) were taken from product lines that were already manufactured for other ranges. Take for example the engines, as both factories already had suitable power-plants in production. Ford of Britain had several possible contenders from their range of vehicles. While the German Ford factory produced among others the Hummer.

Thus it was proposed that the new models would be fitted with different engines, those from Koln would have German-designed engines, whilst the British models would be fitted with the engines built at Dagenham. Meanwhile, the body design requirements were incorporated into styling sketches and these were eventually transformed into a three dimensional clay model. This was further modified and when the design had been finalised, and costs determined the project was then handed over to the engineering team.

The Chief Engineer, Fred Ray, was responsible for chassis design and development but he was already committed to the new D Series range of trucks. A range that was to replace the Thames Trader in 1965. Accordingly, a great deal of the responsibility for the Transit (code-named Redcap at this time),was passed to Vernon Preston.

The body design and development came under the responsibility of Chief Body Engineer Don Ward, whose design centre was still based at the old Briggs Motor Body Works at Dagenham. Ford had taken over this company in 1958, among the more famous contributions that Briggs had made to the British Motor industry that this company produced were the bodies for the Ford Pilot models. Interestingly, by starting out life at Briggs, the Transit project pre-dated Ford's new research and engineering centre at Dunton.

From the outset it was considered essential to offer either petrol or diesel engines, and the British-built petrol engines to be used were a 1664cc 60° V4 OHV unit with a bore and stroke of 93.67mm x 60.35mm fitted with a manual choke. Alternatively the 1621cc four-cylinder Perkins 4.99 engine was offered as a diesel option, although this was soon increased to 1,760cc unit with a slight increase in the bore size. All models were fitted with a synchromesh gearbox, with four forward gears.

Although both engines were reasonably compact, the body design team found it necessary, to make a slightly alternative re-designed front end and bonnet for the models that were to be powered by the slightly more cumbersome diesel engines, This re-designed area gave the diesel-powered models a rather chunkier look with a more pronounced square radiator grille.

Top Right: *From its very first conception, the Transit became a very popular choice as a basis for conversion into motor-homes. Produced by a variety of coachbuilders, either using the basic van or completely custom built from the chassis-cab or chassis-cowl options. These gave the luxury of a vehicle that could be used on a day to day basis just like a car, and at the same time be instantly used as a holiday home, or used for a short weekend break.*

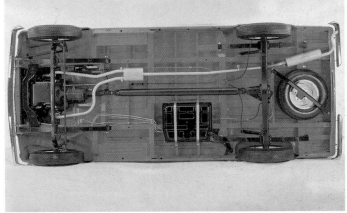

Middle Right: *A very interesting view of a short wheel-base Transit van, and one that the majority of people would not ordinarily see. This illustration shows the substantial, yet lightweight structure of the under-frame, and just how simple maintenance would be for the owner/driver and home mechanic. Obviously, the various truck models were very different being built as they were, with strong chassis.*

Bottom Right: *Here is the superb Ford 2.4 litre diesel that was used to power many of the Transits after the Perkins engine was dropped. The engine had a displacement of 2360cc and produced 61bhp at 3600rpm.*

One of the basic ideas behind the bodyshell design was to avoid the common mistake of building a van and then try and see what they could fit inside. Rather, the Pan-European concept was to take a typical load-space and build a van around it. The accessibility and ease of loading for the interior would indeed become critical, especially with the standardisation of the size of pallets that was then being formulated. Another consideration was the vehicle's ability to be able to carry an 8' x 4' sheet of plywood on the floor of the van between the wheel arches. Side and rear loading were also paramount features, and in its design the Transit team looked at great loading success stories from the 1950s, such as the Austin K8 Three-Way van, whilst avoiding the mistakes of rear-engined vehicles (which had no full height access doors) like the VW Transporter.

The cab was also a crucial part of the design brief, and having decided that the engine would be situated in its own external area, it was possible to isolate unnecessary noise from the cab. An additional benefit came from the fact that the cab would also be able to seat three abreast in a greater degree of comfort. Furthermore, when offered as a chassis-cab or chassis-cowl model for the specialist body builders, the layout could be used to provide a very commodious walk-thru van.

The specialist body trade was a market that had been dominated by the Bedford CA for 13 years when the Transit was launched, and Ford naturally wanted its new model to gain a major share of this sector. The price of the chassis models was very favourable and looked artificially low, which suggests that Ford were determined to beat the opposition at all costs. Their nice flat chassis and relatively small wheels, which did not protrude too deeply into the new rear bodies, were especially appreciated by the specialist builders, whilst the smart front end looked very neat as the pictures in this book show.

Top Left: *When the option of having a 'walk-thru' van body was chosen, the high top Transit was ideal for the express parcel trade or use as mobile shops.*

Middle Left: *When Ford offered their long-wheelbase Transit mini-buses, they instantly proved their worth. A brace of 1969/70 models are seen here in use by Longleat Safari Park, as this variation on a Zebra crossing illustrates.*

Bottom Left: *Although British production of the Ford Transit was moved to the massive Southampton plant. Here members of the Ford management team celebrate the 100,000th Transit built in Britain in less than three years.*

Compared with a modern day Transit, the original models seem rather Spartan but let us not forget that because of continual gradual evolution, it is rather difficult to allow for the fact that we are talking about a design that was inspired more than 40 years ago now. Britain at this time still had something of a motorcar industry too, and a 1965 contemporary of the Transit was the Rolls Royce Silver Shadow model. This was the luxury car maker's first car to be built using a unit-constructed body shell, whilst James Bond found he could swap his Aston Martin DB5 for the brand new DB6. For lesser mortals Ford offered its new Corsair V4, Daihatsu introduced the first Japanese to Britain with the ill-fated Compagno and the Triumph 1300 was previewed in October. At the time of its launch a Silver Shadow would cost £6,670, while the most expensive Ford Transit, a 22-cwt custom minibus with a diesel engine would cost £997.

Above: *The Ford Transit became widely used by both sides of the law during the 1960s and 1970s (just watch an episode of the* Sweeney *if you want to see how much), and they became known as the 'cops and robbers' vans. To this, one might add 'robbed', as they were widely used by various security companies involved in the bulk transfer of cash between businesses and banks. Wearing the yellow and green livery of Security Express, this 1972 example was just one of many Transits modified for this role.*

At the time of its launch, the Transit was very much in advance of its peers. For instance, from the outset they were designed to be fitted with seat-belts of a three-anchor point design, a full four years before the fitting of seatbelts was to became a legal requirement in Britain.

Above: This 1968 MkI long-wheelbase minibus, clearly shows the intelligent way of making the alternative front used on the diesel engine vehicles as cost effective as possible. One can see at a glance that, except for the rather pronounced panel between the front wings and the bonnet, the build is the same. The very early Transits had the circular indicators divided in two as the side-lights were in the upper hemisphere. This particular vehicle (SWY 617F) was converted for the Holmfirth coach operator (Baddeley Brothers) by the Deansgate Motor Company of Manchester and fitted with twelve coach seats. These seats were full size coach seats of the type used by Yeates Coachbuilders in Loughborough. Note the adventurous style of the two-tone green paintwork. Alan Earnshaw

Internally, a very simple yet practical dashboard could be seen through the three-spoke steering wheel, and the instrument binnacle was comprised of a single multi-functional circular dial. Most of the dial was taken up by the clear white figures on the speedometer which registered both mph and kph and a total distance recorder. At regular distances around the speedometer were the small four warning lights for the oil pressure, direction indicator, main beam, and alternator/ignition. The lower area of the dial held the fuel and water temperature gauges. The small knob for the manual choke was fitted to the dashboard to the left of the steering wheel. While to the right of the driver were the windscreen wiper controls, the ignition switch and the light switch; the direction indicator being a column mounted lever on the right which was also the combined head lamp flasher, main beam and horn control.

Windscreen washers were actually operated by a foot switch which was located to the left of the clutch pedal. A slight variation would be found in the instrumentation of the diesel-powered vehicles, but the principle layout of these early models would be very similar. The gear-lever was floor-mounted on the drivers left with the four forward positions and reverse guide being clearly illustrated.

The new Transit was simple and practical, but this was after-all a time when commercial vehicles were designed principally from a functional point of view. Yet, versatility was the key objective for these new commercial vehicles from Ford. They were available as a basic van, a side window model, a pick-up truck or in chassis-cab/cowl variants. Customers were offered a choice of two wheelbase lengths, which shared one of two common front ends depending on the type of engine.

Although the bodyshell came in two lengths, to the uninitiated they looked the same. However, customers did have the option of either hinged or sliding doors for the cab. They also had the option of having a side loading door, whilst the rear of the van could be specified with either twin doors or a top-hinged tailgate. The smaller of the two Transits were the 106" short-wheelbase LCX models, which were designed for payloads of 12-, 17- or 22-cwt. Then came the heavier 118" wheelbase LCY models that had twin rear wheels as standard, and they could carry payloads of 25-, 30-, or 35-cwt.

By the following year, both wheelbase variants were in full production, but customers then had the added choice of either a normal or high roof. Apart from these factory-built commercial vehicles, there were also nine-, 12- and 15-seat minibuses coming off the production line with either longitudinal bench seats or standard transverse seating. The first British-built Ford Transit came down the production line at Langley on 9th August 1965. With a selling price starting at £542 for a 12-cwt swb van, Ford's share of the medium commercial market rapidly increased to 20% and waiting lists grew.

Top Right: *A modest face-lift was incorporated by the adoption of a revised radiator grille for the 1971 season. The pale blue custom van model illustrated here, had the optional fitting of sliding cab doors.*

Middle Right: *A far greater capacity was achieved for carrying light but bulky loads when the customer stipulated the high-top van. The high roof section was manufactured in glass fibre (GRP), whilst the top-hinged tail-gate was an option to the conventional twin rear doors.*

Bottom Right: *During the early 1970s, it was possible to order a long-wheelbase model with single wheels on the rear axle for the carriage of long, yet lightweight loads. This was obviously a saving on unnecessary tyre wear. In this illustration we can clearly see the flange which replaced the rather prominent mudguards used on the twin-wheel versions.*

The next five years were a period of slow, but steady progress, with progressive refinements and improvements going on throughout. The rival Bedford CA by this time was 15-years-old, and it was looking more and more dated. Bedford had been caught with their pants down, sitting back and resting on their laurels due to the seemingly invincible sales on the CA. Successor models the CB to CE had all come to nothing, and the new CF of 1969 turned out to be an American-inspired panel van that spent its life playing catch-up with the Transit. The offerings from BMC/British Leyland the J series and later the Sherpa were no real threat, and neither were the Commer/Dodge offerings from the Rootes Group.

Nevertheless, during 1971 the Transit models were given a face-lift, they now featured a new, more car-like radiator grille although the wings with their lower styling sculptures remained the same. Also at this time came a new model nomenclature, which was essential as the British Government had just introduced metrication system to this country. Reflecting this change Ford Transit model numbers now described their payload capacities in kilograms divided by ten, hence the new 100L model long-wheelbase models of 1974 would be capable of carrying 1,000kg. These long-wheelbase models utilised single wheels on the rear axle and had a flush fitting panel incorporated into the bodywork, rather than the prominent wheel arches over the twin wheel models.

Top Left: *The Transit became one of the most versatile ranges of vehicles ever produced and many private owners lavished a great deal of care and attention on them. One such example that appears to have had an easy life has been custom-painted in an Arabian theme on subtle metallic red background. Note that the driver has entered into the spirit of things also.*

Middle Left: *Although the Transit was primarily a work-horse, they did have many leisure uses, particularly as 'camper-vans' and minibuses. These were ideal for an instant economical family holiday or weekend break. The view here of a minibus though shows a vehicle that was destined to venture further afield than the English coast.*

Bottom Left: *Several different conversions were carried out on basic vans to convert them into motor-caravans. To quote Shakespeare "Rough winds do shake the darling buds of May, and summers lease hath all too short a date." Yet many families made the most of the weather with their very own Transit motorhome.*

In 1972 the Perkins diesel engines that had been offered in the range from the outset, were replaced by Ford's own York 2.4 high-speed diesel engine units. These were a brand new design using a Ricado Comet indirect injection fuel combustion system. Many of the features of these engines were novel at the time; for instance, the valve gear and fuel injection pump, were driven off the crankshaft by a toothed rubber belt rather than a chain. Also the undersides of the pistons were cooled by oil jets, a system normally used on much larger engines than these. Two versions of the engine were introduced these produced either 54 or 61bhp depending on which was chosen.

During the 1970s diesel fuel was far cheaper than petrol and this made diesel engine vehicles of this class extremely popular. Very soon Ford found that over 50% of Transit sales were diesel-powered. In an effort to further improve fuel economy, Ford's British engineering team, designed a new direct injection diesel engine.

Above: *Here Penthouse Racing adapts a comparatively low-key project with a Transit van in a simple, yet sombre livery. However, by using a little glamour, an extremely eye-catching marketing method is achieved. This particular model is a long-wheel base.*

The key to the success of this power plant was the new high pressure fuel injection system, which used a high speed rotary pump developed by Lucas. This new 2.5Di engine improved fuel consumption by 15%. Further refinement to the Transit range came in 1972, including the fitting of front wheel disc-brakes. The year also marked the start of production of the Transit at the new Southampton factory.

Ford also celebrated the sale of the millionth Transit to be built and sold since production began. This was actually a short-wheelbase engine minibus with a two-litre engine, which was destined for Nigeria.

Above: *Not quite designed to the same high quality standards as some of the high profile racehorse transporters. Yet these vehicles built upon Transit chassis would ensure a safe and comfortable journey for going to the dogs.*

The year 1976, saw the introduction of the new 3.5 tonne models, which were introduced to take full advantage of the legislative break-point affecting the fitting of tachograph equipment to record driver's hours, and licences of commercial vehicle operators. Always well shod, having radial tyres all round from its launch, more improvements were made in 1976 to cater for the increased weights now being carried. From that year on new steel-ply tyres and ventilated front disc brakes became standard fittings.

There was also a Transit for the roughest terrain, as a four-wheel drive conversion became available. In this guise it saw use in civil engineering, the emergency services, forestry work, building and allied trades, public utility undertakings (power, gas, telephones and water) and even in the military.

For the standard drive models, their use was voluminous, with (once again) the emergency services of ambulance, fire, and police all putting them to good use. In fact, if you think about it, all of our lives have been touched in some way by a Transit, perhaps it was the vehicle that carried your expectant mother to the maternity hospital, or carried the mail order baby items ordered by your parents. At the other end of the life scale, the Transit has again been widely used as an emergency ambulance, for mortuary work and even as a hearse.

Between birth and death, we have all found the Transit to be part of our lives, even if this fact has not been consciously recognised. They have arrived at our doors with the morning post or express parcels, they have been used in public service vehicle fleets, and they have even called to collect our rubbish. The Transit has carried newspapers and magazines, sold us ice-cream, delivered the daily pint of milk, carried millions of workmen on their daily chores and delivered the products of thousands of manufacturing business. Indeed, their popularity has become so great that you can now be almost guaranteed that you can see one on almost any road or street in the land.

The success of the Marque can only be down to three things, the first being the original concept of building a van around a useful load space, the second being the consultations with dealers, drivers, mechanics and operator, with the final one being the continual refinement of the range in line with developing demands and past experience.

To say that this forward thinking approach was both justified and an outstanding success is rather an understatement. For within a very short time of its introduction, the Transit became the leader in its field and has stayed there un-assailed for 40-years. There cannot be any greater testimony, to the economy, reliability and versatility of the Transit range than this.

Below: *The fact that Transit models are a common sight on Britain's roads, look at this example in a typical British street scene. With its traditional London Transport Leyland Titan RTL model bus, which is being passed by a Bedford TK five-ton van in the bright yellow Lucozade livery, nothing looks out of place, especially the Transit. Closer examination reveals that this vehicle is actually a left-hand-drive European model, which is destined for a dog food suppliers at Langesø in Denmark and was probably photographed for publicity purposes before being exported.*

Above: *The 1977 Ford Transit shown in this photograph is really little more than a very flamboyant, and eye-catching exercise in advertising.*

In addition to those people who are familiar with the various styles and applications of Ford Transits that have been produced in Britain and Europe during the past four decades a high percentage of them will have driven, or ridden in a Ford Transit at some time. Many of us have had use of them on a regular basis over a long period of time. This is particularly true of the staff here at Trans-Pennine Publishing for I know that my Editor, Alan Earnshaw, has driven numerous van and minibus versions. Included in the list was the Fell-Runner Minibus services, which operated a voluntary service through the villages at the edge of Cumbria's fells, carrying locals and holiday-makers alike behind a reliable Transit.

Meanwhile the Production Manager, Matthew Richardson, has often driven one of the chassis-only examples of the Transit, which was fitted with custom-built bodywork (vintage style) for Ringtons Tea. Personally I have driven various Transit panel vans and Luton vans and was for a long time employed as the driver of a Transit minibus that operated all over the north and west of Cumbria.

If you have not personally driven one yourself, the chances are that you will know plenty of people who have. Quite rightly, when the Transit celebrated its 30th anniversary in 1995, it was being dubbed as 'The Backbone of Britain', by using a slogan that featured in a TV commercial to the backing of the catching Slade tune of *Coz I Luv You*. In themselves, the lyrics of this song from the Glamrock era of the early-1970s were quite appropriate, as the Transit had by then literally become Britain's best-loved van.

Above: *Prior to the introduction of the Ford Transit, in what was a Pan-European venture, the British and German Ford manufacturing plants were producing their own individual range of vehicles in this payload category. This superb photograph illustrating part of the fleet of Monark Television and radio service vans clearly shows examples of the type of Ford Taunus. These were known as the FK models and were built in the factory at Koln.*

Right: *The British Ford factory was producing commercial vehicles of a similar size, and of the same forward control layout as the German-built Taunus. These were known as the Ford Thames 400E and were offered in the standard van layout, Dormobile, pick-up truck or as a chassis-cab for the fitting of specialist bodywork.*

Above: *Quite simple motor caravan conversions of the basic Ford Transit vans were carried out by various companies from 1965 onwards. When fitted with the option of an elevating roof these made ideal holiday accommodation, yet they were also still very handy for conventional everyday use as a large family estate car or general runabout.*

Left: *This excellent photograph from 1972 shows the later and more simple style of radiator grille used on the first type of Transit models. Wings and bonnet remained largely the same though. This Transit 90 model had the fitted option of a high-top, which was constructed in durable yet lightweight fibre-glass. This van also had the top-hinged tailgate as an alternative to the two rear doors. All-in-all, a package which allowed very generous load space and ease of loading too.*

Above: *For basic conversions the panel van body could be adapted for a variety of purposes, but for really special applications a body-builder needed the 'blank canvas' of the chassis-cab or chassis-cowl options. Here a stylish, much more accommodating 'camper-van' has been created by Travelhome with their MkIII model.*

Right: *Here we see a MkII Transit bus based on the long-wheelbase chassis. This view shows the principle styling heritage of the original 1965 model but with streamlining revisions. The most obvious being the new wing line, bonnet and radiator grille. Also prominent was the de-chroming exercise; the bumpers, radiator grille and light bezels were now black. Not only did this give the re-vamped models a new crisp look, but succeeded in its role as an aid to maintenance.*

Above: *In this official posed photograph we have an illustration of the Transit short-wheelbase bus with a normal height roof. These were ideal vehicles for works transport, sports and social clubs or even just everyday transport for the larger family. Note will be made of the increased window area over the previous models, as will the larger wrap-round bumpers and the headlamp wash system.*

Left: *Even further development work took place on the important issues of increased fuel economy and driver safety. The new Transits when they were introduced were further examples of continual development. Not only was the window area further increased but as on this model the front bumper incorporates fog lights. To celebrate 40 years of Transit production the Hallmark was created as a special edition.*

THE MkII FORD TRANSIT

Launched in March 1978, came the MkII models of the Ford Transit. These had an almost complete styling change, yet still maintained that instant 'Transit look'. The bonnets were wider, lengthened and more streamlined, allowing the same bodyshell to be fitted with either petrol or diesel engines.

The front wings were completely redesigned, and followed the contours of the bonnet. They no longer retained the square housing of the headlight bezels, for the headlights were now situated in the outer ends of a simple black radiator grille. This wrap-round grille was actually situated on a higher plane than previously, whilst small auxiliary vents were located between the grille and the new style bumper.

Above: *Seen against an impressive back drop, we see one of the new MkII models. From this profile vantage point, whilst there was a lot in common with the earlier model, the Mk II had new wings and bonnet design. This allowed for the fitment of either the petrol or the diesel engine variant in the same shell. Also new at this time were more fuel efficient 1.6 and 2.0 litre OHC petrol engines and Ford's own C3 automatic transmission.*

The former circular indicator flashers that were previously set below the headlights were gone also and these were replaced by narrow, tall oblong units that were situated in the leading edge of the front wings, but adjacent to the headlights in the radiator grille.

29

On the new MkII, the bonnet, wings and radiator grille all had a more uniform and harmonious visual appeal. For a start, the fitting of chrome-plated items, such as handles and trim was then discontinued. Thereafter, the radiator grilles, bumpers, wing mirrors, windscreen wiper arms, door handles, and even the windscreen surround were black, in an effort to make these new models as 'low maintenance' effective as possible.

Back in 1972, two Ford Transits had been used as proving beds for the new 2.4-litre York diesel engine. These being a short-wheelbase van and a 12-seat minibus, which established three new world records in seven days during day and night driving around Italy's famous Monza race track. The van covered 10,000km at an average speed of 75mph, while the bus was driven 10,000 miles at an average speed of 73.7mph. This exercise proved the worth of these new diesel engines so much so, that by 1977 Transit sales in Italy accounted for 28.6% of all van sales in that country. All of these Transits were powered by the new 2.4-litre engine too.

The more fuel efficient 1.6-litre, Kent petrol engines were introduced to the range during 1975, and these replaced the long serving 1.7-litre V4 Essex engines. Later in the decade, Ford's C3 automatic transmission was introduced as an option to the manual gearbox, upholding the high standard of customer satisfaction that the original Transit models had secured in the market right from their initial launch.

Top Left: *The universal appeal of the Transit could have been rather daunting to the designers when the time arrived for modernisation of this best seller. In the event, the MkII models were a very well executed design, combining the familiar look of the original, with just a dash of a styling modernity and improved specification. Note the combination of slam doors for the cab and a sliding side door.*

Middle Left: *Problems with the new Bedford CF chassis used in ambulance work during the mid-1970s gave the Transit a very clear advantage in the market place. Here a MkII version is seen in the employ of the Scottish Ambulance Service, but note the drab austerity of the NHS buildings behind it.*

Bottom Left: *This long-wheelbase MkII Transit (CYV 876V), equipped with a huge telescopic beacon, served as a divisional control unit with F Division of the London Fire Brigade. The chequered band along the body side and on the front wing emphasises the newer styling applied to the MkII model.*
London Fire Brigade

The new MkII continued to offer a wide variety of carrying capacity. Furthermore, they had such a commendable choice of body styles and transmission systems that it was almost impossible for a customer not to find a model that suited their business perfectly. The MkII variants continued what had started in 1965, but they also introduced a greater level of dependability to the range. An example of this would be in the protection that was offered to the bodyshell from the MkII onwards

By the very nature of the many roles that light commercial vehicles fulfil, they are more prone to corrosion and damage than private cars. In an effort to counteract this almost natural problem, Ford had introduced their cathodic anti-corrosion programme during 1979. Winter driving conditions, around this time too, were made much more comfortable by the fitting of more powerful and efficient heaters with car-like ducts.

Above: *During 1978, after 13-years of production, the Ford Transit received the first really significant facelift. Our photograph here shows that, with just a half bulkhead behind the driver's seat, easy access could be afforded to the sales area of this 1979 ice-cream van body, which was done by Archibald Scott of Bellshill for Marchetti Brothers.*

Braking was yet another area to be improved, and the MkII had a much more positive response than the earlier models. In 1980 petrol engine models received a variable venture carburettor and thermo viscous fan fitted to the engines. Then, within a few months, a new cylinder-head was developed for use with liquid petroleum gas. After extensive testing and development, this became an option that could be fitted to the 2.0 litre DOHC petrol engine models from 1981.

Above: *The Transit has proved to be an extremely popular form of transport for many entertainers over the years. Many groups have used them for transporting group members and instruments. Several even owning minibus versions.*

Introduced in April 1984 was Ford's own Dagenham-built 2.5-litre direct injection diesel engine, which had a rotary fuel injection pump. This system utilised the principle of having fuel injected directly into the cylinder by a high-pressure pump, rather than the previous method of having the fuel injected into a pre-chamber using a low-pressure pump. This significantly increased power over the existing unit, while at the same time fuel consumption was improved by 15%. This new engine benefited from the experience gained on the design of the York engine which had been introduced during January 1972.

Retrospectively, many people will point out the faults of the York engine, and indeed there were quite a number of valid criticisms of it. The York engine however, had been a very successful power plant, for by the time production ended more than 625,000 had been built. Indeed, these York engines were so well engineered that apart from the addition of glowplugs in 1978 they had remained unchanged throughout their production span. However, times had changed, and owner/operator/driver expectations had changed dramatically during the 1970s,

Something new was needed for the 1980s, and exceptional engineering talent from Ford would eventually bring about what was effectively a brand new replacement. Indeed, apart from the pushrods that operated the valves and the camshaft rear cover plate, nothing else was carried over from the York design. This complete re-think was not only a response to greater demands, but it was also a boost to customer confidence as well.

During the following year, another remarkable milestone for the Ford Motor Company was achieved when the two-millionth Transit model rolled off the production lines. This was indeed a reason for celebration. Remarkably this had been achieved in just 20-years of manufacture, and it emphasised the high regard customers had for these vehicles. The actual vehicle was a long-wheelbase minibus and was handed over to the well known conservationist and television personality Dr. David Bellamy at the Southampton plant in Britain on 25th July1985.

During 1985, engineering emphasis began to address the problem of exhaust emission control, as increasing legislation was aimed towards the health problems associated with carbon-monoxide in the atmosphere; thus work was started on low-emission engines. These engines introduced a number of small changes, which were arrived at after a breakthrough in a better understanding of the direct injection system and resulting modification of the engines.

These 'cleaner' engines now had a new combustion system with a re-entrant bowl depression combustion chamber in the piston. Also new were the 'slim tip' Stanadyne diesel injectors and the introduction of exhaust gas re-circulation (EGR). These new engines went into production during 1988 and they were marketed by Ford as the 'green movement' and environmental concern swept across Europe.

The considerable advanced technical achievements on these engines was recognised immediately when the Ford Motor Company was awarded a German energy conservation award, and before long this was very soon being followed by a similar British Design Council Award, both of which set a mark of approval on Ford's efforts.

Top Right: *The well respected conservationist and TV personality, Dr David Bellamy is seen here at the home of the Ford Transit in Southampton on 25th July 1985. David is receiving the keys to a long-wheelbase minibus, the two-millionth Transit to be built.*

Bottom Right: *Although Bedford, the now sadly missed British commercial vehicle manufacturer, had the justifiable boast "You see them everywhere", even they did not get as far as the moon. Despite the picture conveying another impression, Ford didn't manage it either and this unique Ford Transit van was firmly down to earth. Note the six custom wheels, and high-back seats and the gull-wing door, there is also an observation area at the rear, and globe skylights; however, the paint work is out of this world.*

While on the subject of publicity stunts, it is worth mentioning that Ford built a Transit named the Supervan. Principally, it was designed as a test bed for new engines, but as a publicity exercise this high profile vehicle made its debut at Brands Hatch on Easter Monday 1971. Although employing a Transit van bodyshell, it was actually based on the Ford GT 40, and was powered by a five-litre V8 engine, meaning it could reach an astonishing 150mph.

Below: *Models of the Transit fulfilled roles with police and security services around the world, but as the issues of crowd control grew worse during the 1980s, more protection had to be added to the basic models, Here a left-hand-drive has been equipped with mesh window guards as well as barred headlamps and indicators.*

It is reported that one eminent journalist from one of the leading sports car magazines of the day was allowed out in the Supervan to observe it through its paces, and when coming through a chicane commented that the steering seemed very light at that time. To this the Ford driver who was accompanying him answered, in a matter of fact way, that the reason for this was that the front wheels were off the track at that time.

The Transit Supervan was obviously, absolutely the most remarkable vehicle clothed in the Transit bodyshell, with its astonishing performance. Yet even this vehicle became overshadowed during 1985, when Supervan II made its debut. This again was based on another Ford ex-Le mans racing car, this time the C100, which was powered by a DFY Cosworth V8 engine. Supervan II managed to achieve a speed of 174 mph on the Silverstone track.

Later still during 1995, the Transit Super Van III would emerge after a period of continual development. This was styled on the same body structures as the Mark III Transit with its aerodynamic wedge nose style, but using the later oval style of radiator grille that was fitted at that time. .

Based on a short-wheelbase, low roof van, but mounted low on the chassis to improve stability and drag factor, Supervan III was fitted with a tailgate that was cut away to allow the exhaust system to breath. An aero-foil was fitted to the rear roof area, and a front spoiler was also fitted again to aid with the overall streamlining. Supervan III, like the previous Supervan II, was powered by a Cosworth engine. This was a 3.5-litre HB, F1 V8 engine, which was mounted in the load area over the rear axle. It produced a spectacular 650bhp at 13,000rpm, and continued the use of the Supervan as a publicity tool.

Above: *The second supervan excercise. Supervan II is seen going through its paces as it hurries around the track,*
.

In the general market Ford continued to gain praise for the attributes of the various Transit models, mainly thanks to their performance, reliability, engineering excellence, and the input of the latest technology. The Supervan may have been a good publicity stunt, but it was functionality that mattered to those who bought the model. Ford therefore used both their own publicity exercises and various journalists to keep the Transit in the news. For instance, freelance journalist Simon Harvey, under the careful observation of the RAC, drove a short-wheelbase Transit carrying a half tonne payload on a complete circuit of the M25 at an average speed of 50.2mph with a creditable 40mpg average fuel consumption.

THE MкIII TRANSIT

During 1986, Ford introduced the new Transit, code-named the VE6, which stood for Van for Europe Project 6. This new model was a complete revision of energy efficiency. The most noticeable of these being a completely new streamlined cab, which not only increased fuel economy but also greatly increased cabin space. The bonnet was now on the same profile as the windscreen and effectively produced a drag coefficient factor of just 0.37 and this bettered a lot of cars that were in production at the time. This resulted in better fuel economy and savings of up to 8% were recorded. The smoother air-flow nose, incorporated crumple zones, but at the same time came far better visibility. Much larger window glass area was incorporated into the design with not only a bigger windscreen, but also larger doors with much increased side windows.

Above: *The third generation of the Transit appeared to have a far more boxy profile bodily, although many said it looked more bland. Internally it was more commodious than the previous models, providing a greater degree of load-space. The cabin area gained an ultra-modern look with a greater aerodynamic nose. Pictured here are just a handful of the various models in the range.*

The bonnet was now also longer and wider, which afforded far better engine access. A simple black slatted radiator grille was incorporated into the design and new, larger headlights and indicators all helped to harmonise the new look. Larger and more effective wrap-round bumpers were also an added safety feature. Better, flush-fitting door handles (complete with Chubb locks) were a further improvement, whilst the lockable fuel filler cap was now re-sited just behind the passenger cab door.

Completely revised body strengthening swage lines also added to the ultra-modern look, but the real strength of the new design came in the fact that it now allowed a far greater increase in load-space. This increase was between 11 and 13.5%, depending on which model was purchased and it came as a real added bonus. Easier loading was achieved with wider and taller rear doors. The dimensions of the side door were also increased at this time, and the apperture could accept a one-metre wide pallet. Although a high-roof was only available initially on the long-wheelbase version, this was also to become an option on the short-wheelbase models too the following year.

A major re-design of the underbody structure, allowed these new Transits to withstand the newly introduced 30mph crash barrier test. During 1988, Ford introduced their MT75 five-speed gearbox. Power steering was also offered as an option on the long-wheelbase models, a full year ahead of its being made available on the short-wheelbase models. The following year, Ford expanded the range even further with the introduction of the Executive minibus, while a low roof 12-seat minibus also appeared in the Ford Transit line-up.

Top Right: *This crew-cab pick-up truck shows just how much cabin space could be specified, as six men could be carried in a vehicle that still had a generous load space. Yet because of the far larger glass area, these models were far less claustrophobic than they might have been. What is more, they were an improvement over many other manufacturer's models that were on the market at that time. Crew-cab vehicles proved very popular particular with building and engineering trades.*

Middle Right: *Illustrated here we have a view of one of the basic Transit panel vans. Notice from this view how airy the cabin area appears to be, along with the effective and harmonious styling of the air-intakes that are incorporated into the bonnet design. This tidy example is in the owners' simple overall red livery and parked outside their premises on an industrial estate in Workington, Cumbria. Newlands are a company renowned for the manufacture and fitting of blinds.*

Bottom Right: *Young members of the CND campaign look on from the distance as the actor Michael Caine casually poses alongside the new Ford Transit. The introduction of the wedge-shaped model in the mid-1980s was a complete re-design of what would eventually prove to be, the most popular range of light commercial, which is beaten only in its longevity by the Volkswagen Transporter range.*

Above: *This guy is not in too much danger of falling off his perch, even though he is 'breaking the law' by not wearing a seatbelt. Employing a chassis-cab model with a specialist body built on the back, Capital Radio used this unique way of bringing the entertainment medium of the radio to the notice of the travelling public.*

To commemorate 25 years of continual production of the Transit, Ford introduced their Silver Jubilee model in 1990; these were based on the 100 standard van models, but were painted in a metallic silver colour scheme and fitted with unique wheel trims. During 1991, Ford received even greater acclaim for their diesel research and technology when they introduced their VE-64 models, these were fitted with the first ever turbocharged version of the 2.5-litre engine.

This was the first medium commercial to use the electronic timing and metering fuel system. Furthermore, this engine was also able to meet the tough emission legislation that was starting to be enforced on motor vehicle manufacturers during the late-1980s. At the heart of this new version of the 2.5-litre engine was the Lucas Diesel Systems EPIC (Electronically Programmed Injection Control) fuel injection system.

This was known as the drive-by-wire engine control whereby the accelerator was not directly connected to the engine but quite simply controlled by a wire that relayed a signal to the engine according to the position of the accelerator pedal. This system, along with other readings taken from around the engine would all provide a much more accurate level of fuel consumption control. Other makers were inspired by the system, including Land Rover who fitted it to their 2.5Di engines.

Launched in 1993 came a new heavyweight derivative of the Ford Transit, this being the 230 model, which had a gross vehicle weight of 3,995kg. These 230 models were developed by Ford's Special Vehicle Engineering Department in response for requests for a heavier chassis. One big fleet user in the UK became British Telecom, another was the AA.

All Transit models were updated in 1994, and whilst looking structurally the same, there were quite a number of both internal and external changes. The most obvious of these was the adoption of an oval radiator grille, which was introduced to bring the vans and light commercial vehicles in line with the family of Ford cars that were in production at the time.

Other changes incorporated a reduction on interior noise levels, a new climate control system and upgrades to the safety and security specifications. A revision of cab comfort was also undertaken, resulting in a completely new car-like interior and dashboard. The Transit then became the first medium commercial vehicle range to offer as standard fittings driver and front seat passenger airbags, seatbelt grabbers, seatbelt pre-tensioners, and anti-submarining seat pans. They were also one of the first of manufacturers in this class of vehicle to fit three point seat belts for the front centre passenger. New 2.5-litre diesel engines with improved emission control were also produced at this time, and this was also the year that the three-millionth Transit was manufactured.

Top Right: *Transits have proved their worth across the wide spectrum of light commercial vehicle usage. The motoring organisations have, and continue to use them extensively, particularly the larger well known ones. This posed view shows an AA Relay unit. Note will be taken that Ford made use of a competitive manufacturers car to play the role of the"stricken" vehicle on the cradle, in this roadside drama.*

Middle Right:*This Transit truck shows the generous load area that was offered in the long-wheelbase format. Also worthy of note is provision of a headlight wash system, quite a boon on vehicles used in the building trades. Curiously, although this vehicle is British-registered it is a left-hand-drive model.*

Bottom Right: *Always in the forefront with new ideas and the latest technology, Ford were never slow to expand their market. Hence one new idea was the option of crew-cab vans. These vehicles offered safe and comfortable accommodation for five, with entry via the cabin or the side door, plus a large area of load space too.*

Top Left: *From the very beginning of the planning stages for the Transit models, Ford aimed these vehicles at the lucrative emergency service vehicle market. Taking it by storm the company found that it had the desired knock-on effect that their products could almost sell themselves. This actual vehicle, as the registration suggests was a demonstrator for the ambulance services and is seen in a posed publicity picture as opposed to actual service conditions.*

Middle Left: *Because of the engine being fitted in its own bonnet area, the Ford Transit soon found itself in demand for being fitted as parcel vans, mobile shops and ice-cream vans. This example was pictured whilst attending a car-boot sale at South Church near Bishop Auckland, County Durham during the warm summer of 2004.* Author's collection

Bottom Left: *Also found in the back streets of Bishop Auckland, this time during 2005, our view shows a late model MkIII Transit. This van (X81 NGE) is included here just slightly out of chronological sequence to illustrate the very subtle differences of the bodywork in these face-lift models. The most obvious change of all is the new style of oval grille that was employed to give the commercial vehicles a common appearance with the Ford car range.* Author's collection

The Transit range was further expanded by the introduction of a new 17-seat long-wheelbase minibus in 1996. This model had the highest level of safety incorporated into any comparable vehicle at this time and was equipped to meet the new stringent health and safety laws introduced by the Department of Transport. These new laws applied to every minibus that would be used to transport children to and from school, or on organised trips. This new legislation overturned the former concessions that had allowed three under 14-year-olds to count as two passengers. and stated that each child must thereafter be carried in a forward-facing seat fitted with an approved seat belt on all trips. This legislation applied to all buses and coaches used for transporting school children that were capable of travelling at 60mph. This did not however apply to normal fare stage buses that were used to convey the general public, although regulations would later be tightened on these also.

Rather than design their new 17-seat minibus only to comply with the requested criteria of these new laws, Ford exceeded the necessary requirements. They recognised that the welfare and safety of school children was of the most paramount concern and built such safety features into all their minibuses.

A FACE LIFT

The new minibuses were fitted with three-part inertia reel lap and diagonal seat belts, whilst the seats and the seat fixings were also tested to the same standards as the then current passenger car levels, which was twice the normal level of those required for a bus. They were also fitted with high-back seats that had fixed (see-through) head-restraints, whilst airbags were incorporated into the dash in front of the driver and the outer front seat passenger. The fitting of an electronic engine immobiliser was standard, whilst mandatory equipment such as a first aid kit, fire extinguisher and passenger grab handles and illumination over all the exits were included. Anti-lock brakes became standard fitting as too were the large door mirrors. The interior mirror had enhanced rear vision.

Above: *The Ford Transit has had a long association with the police service and this continued through the MkIII range. This impressive vehicle in the modern reflective 'Battenburg' livery was used by the Lothian & Borders Police force in the role of a Community Policing Vehicle.*

These new Ford Transit minibuses were extremely well equipped, the enlarged range came with factory-fitted seating in four different capacities. Three sizes had long been available, namely 9-, 12- and 15-seat, but the 17-seat variant opened up a new market at a time when larger buses were struggling to sell due to an overall reduction in the demand for travel. Hence the 17-seater soon found itself a new market, in which its comparatively low price of £23,645 to £24,490 appealed to many operators, especially for school or rural bus work.

Above: *Many customers, especially in the parcels delivery or garment trade sectors had the need for a vehicle with a greater load space though not necessarily a greater payload. For these users Ford moved on from the high-top models to develop their 'High-Cube' vans with an extended length and a high roof, which allowed 12 cubic metres of cargo to be carried.*

By the 1990s, the Transit range was offered in a very wide selection of commercial bodies. As well as the conventional vans with the various styles, chassis lengths and engines, Ford were offering the 190 and 230 chassis-cabs and double cab chassis. These models had bodies and payload capacities of 1,802 and 2,297kg respectively, but they were also available with a 709mm frame extension that allowed them to accommodate bodies of up to four metres long.

When the customer choose to buy the 190 or 230 double cab chassis, they were able to accommodate a six-person crew. Those models that were fitted with the double cab, could also be ordered with a chassis extension, but in this case the extension was somewhat shorter and it only allowed for the fitting of bodies up to three metres long.

These chassis -cab trucks could and were used with an even wider range of bodies than the vans. The possibilities were almost endless, small drop-side trucks for engineering, market gardeners, joiners, or general transport work, small tippers for civil engineering and building trades, or box vans and luton vans for light household removals, parcel deliveries or the garment trade. Often the chassis cab format was chosen as the base on which many of the specialist body builders constructed the various styles of motor caravans.

Even the standard panel vans came in a very wide choice range at this time. For instance, in the long-wheelbase sector alone, there were three models that could carry rigid loads as long as 10' 6" (3,214mm) and include a two-person crew, whilst handling a payload of 1,700kg. On these lwb vans a semi-high roof was standard and an 8.4 cubic metre of load-space was available, but when the high roof option was requested, the load space was then as much as 10.0 cubic metres.

These lwb vans were complimented by four short-wheelbase models, which could take loads up to 2,468mm long and had a payload of 1,468kg. These vans were available with the standard roof and either semi-high or a high roof, the largest version of these short-wheelbase vans contained a load-space of 7.9 cubic metres.

Ford introduced their High Cube 230 models during 1995, these were intended for the parcel delivery trades, and were on an extra long platform and used a high roof. These models boasted a payload space of 12 cubic metres, which was an overall increase of 19 per cent increase on the capacity of the previous models. The year 1995, was also the 30th anniversary of the Transit and to celebrate this Ford launched their unique model called the 'Hallmark' these were actually based on the Ford Transit 100 custom van.

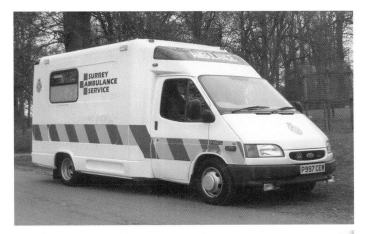

Top Right: *During a Ford press day held at Althorpe, the stately home of the Spencer family, the Trans-Pennine editorial team were invited to put the new Transit range through its paces. Here, Matthew Richardson, the Editorial Production Manager tries out the latest Ford Transit/UVG ambulance around the Northamptonshire countryside in 1996, before the vehicle was handed over to the Surrey Ambulance Service NHS Trust on an extended trial.* Trans-Pennine Archive

Middle Right: *This illustration shows the improved interior of the MkIII Transit on the 190 long-wheelbase model. All the controls are within easy reach of the driver, and the driver's cab feels more like a private car than a commercial vehicle.*

Bottom Right: *Having a low drag factor, the Ford Transits, combined a great carrying capacity with a very commendable performance as this 190 long-wheelbase van on the test track clearly illustrates. Improved, larger glass area and rear-view mirrors all help to instill a great degree of confidence that whatever the weather, or situation that the driver may find themselves in, the new Transit range will be more than up to the job.*

With a mixture of continual development, keeping an eye on the market, customer feed back and awareness of the competition, the Transit range was never slow to adopt the latest technology. Neither was there any slowing down on the constant demand for these extremely versatile commercial vehicles. The range of models was understandably very impressive by 1997. There was a choice of five comprehensively equipped short-wheelbase models, available with normal, semi-high, or high roofs. Meanwhile the long-wheelbase version had six models, which were available in a choice of semi-high and high roof.

As mentioned earlier, chassis-cabs were available either as single or double cab versions, all with a heavy duty ladder frame. But as a more up-market exercise on this theme Ford also produced a fully in-house built pick-up this was known as the 'Flareside', this stylish creation proved very popular with small businesses. Flareside models, were actually based on the short - wheelbase chassis-cab with a payload capacity of one tonne. These were built with double-skinned aluminium sides and a composite load floor, rather in the style of a typical mid-1950s, American pick-up truck.

Mini-buses remained extremely popular with commercial buyers and private buyers. Ford were still offering 9-, 12-, 15-, or 17-seat examples, but a further and more exclusive example on this theme were the two Ford Transit Tourneo models.

Top Left: *The MkIII models were further modernised in 1994 when among the improvements, the slatted radiator grille was replaced with an oval style of radiator grille. This was of similar design to those fitted on to the various cars that Ford were producing at that time and was a deliberate styling feature intended to create a degree of family uniformity right across the range. As an aside, we might mention that during the early 1950s Ford cars were fitted with a chrome airplane style bonnet mascot, the one on this 1994 Transit appears to have come loose.*

Bottom Left: *Such was the instant appeal of the Transit and efficient productivity methods employed, that it has continued to fill its original role of a Van for Europe for four decades. Within 11 years the millionth Transit had been produced, and nine years after that (during its 20th-year in production) the two-millionth was made. Our illustration here confirms that the three-millionth example left the production line on 6th September 1994. It does not take a statistician to work out that Ford were producing around one million Transits every decade, but it does illustrate their exceptional popularity.*

The Transit Tourneo models were actually based on the short-wheelbase minibus, but designed to provide luxurious and exclusive accommodation for either the large-car family buyer as well as commercial enterprise. Spacious, comfortable accommodation was provided for nine people in the Tourneo models, which were both sumptuously furnished and comprehensively equipped, while still being able to offer a very generous amount of luggage accommodation in the rear of the vehicle. A side door with step afforded entrance to the passenger compartment. While at the rear of the vehicle an easily operated tailgate offered a degree of protection when loading or unloading luggage in inclement weather. Standard features for these models included the Safeguard engine immobiliser, power-assisted steering, body-side moulding and colour coded bumpers, also folding third row seats.

Above: *Not only did the various Transit models fulfill their expected roles in commerce and industry, they even aspired to the luxury private car industry. Ford introduced the Tourneo models for those customers requiring large family transport in a more up-market vehicle than a conventional dormobile. Our illustration here shows the luxurious Tourneo GLX.*

In addition there was an even more luxurious version, in the form of the the Tourneo GLX, which offered an even higher degree of luxury and comfort. The GLX models accommodated only eight people, but they did so in even more luxury. In this model the seats were upholstered in velour, most of which featured arm rests. Other benefits included central locking, electric front windows, and electrically-operated and heated door mirrors.

Above: *Ford introduced a further variant to the Transit range for small business users with the Flareside pick-up, which was based on the short wheelbase chassis-cab. They were designed and built with a generous load box constructed of double-skinned aluminium sides and a composite floor. The styling was rather akin to various American pick-up trucks.*

Further engineering improvements aided by new technology continued to be implemented into the Transit range throughout the late-1990s. Indeed, so many innovations and improvements were introduced, we can just take time to consider a few of the highlights in the space we have available.

During 1998 electronic brake force distribution and traction assistance was introduced along with an enhanced immobilisation system and column lock. Around this time Ford had also introduced their Auto-clutch system.

With this system, gears are selected in the normal way with the operation taking place through a conventional gate although the clutch automatically disengages as the gear lever is moved. When sensors in the system tell the control unit that the next gear has been reached this then re-engages the clutch.

Such was the engineering technology and quality during this period, that operating costs were substantially reduced, not only through better fuel consumption but also in servicing. For instance, at this time Transits with petrol engines were expected to operate 12,500 miles between servicing intervals. All the engines that were fitted to the Transits produced in Britain continued to be produced at the Ford factory at Dagenham and the latest master-piece was introduced to the assembly line at the Southampton plant during 1999. This was Ford 115PS unit, a new direct injection diesel engine with turbo-charger and inter-cooling.

During the year 2000, the four-millionth Transit was produced, which was indeed a remarkable achievement as this meant that the previous total of around one-million per decade had been cut in half, with a million being made in just five years. By this time the three principle factories were involved in the manufacture of Transits, these being Southampton, Genk in Belgium and Azambuja in Portugal. However one of the best years for actual total production was 1989, when a total of 173,059 of the various models were completed. The versatile and extremely popular Transit range from that time carried a standard three years/100,000 miles manufacturer's warranty; this was the first time this was offered on any Ford vehicle.

Also during 2000, the first all-new Transit in ten years was introduced to the public. There were now three wheelbase options offered, short, long and now medium. This new Transit was completely redesigned with a slightly more chunky look. Larger windows were fitted and improved security systems were introduced; including key locking, bonnet remote and central/double locking. Meanwhile, the use of peel-resistant bonding to body rear windows as an optional glazing feature, eliminated the use of rubber seals as a greater security feature.

Ford continued their commitment to all aspects of reliability and safety, and equipped the latest Transits with 'generation' seat belts; these were specifically designed with the suitability for adjustments to suit smaller occupants and children. Anti-lock brakes with electronic brake-force distribution, were also a new feature right across the Ford Transit range at this time.

Top Right: *This portrait shot shows that the aero-dynamic design was still a satisfactory feature of the new generation Transit. High-rise bumpers all around offered an excellent degree of protection. A large glass area was a very practical provision from the driver's point of view, yet the bonded windows instill a sensation of complete security.*

Middle Right: *Many people have become attached to their Transit in the same way that individuals feel about a favourite car. Looking at this view of a special edition Silver Blue high-roof van it is not hard to see why. Possibly in 40 years or so, EX 54 HOA, might be a subject for preservation.*

Bottom Right: *Illustrated here is the rear detail of the special Silver Blue model. This view shows details of the substantial, yet unobtrusive, rear bumper and the practical load-step. Also in evidence are the neat stacked light units and the discrete door hinges.*

INTO THE NEW CENTURY, THE MkIV TRANSIT

Ford have continued to improve their range of Transit models in every practical way, and this was clearly emphasised when the year 2000 saw a complete redesign of the model. The three wheel-base lengths could then accommodate load lengths from 2.5- to 4-metres and there was still available the choice of three roof heights, normal, semi-high, and high. In turn, these offered load space capacity of between 5.9 and 12.28 cubic metres. This new van range meant that the customer not only had the largest range of options in commercial vehicles of this class. but almost certainly any other class of vehicles.

Above: *This illustration of the special edition* Silver Blue *model dating from 2004/5 shows how much continual improvement Ford have made on the Transit models through the four decades of its production history.*

Ford now even offered the choice of front or rear wheel drive and this unique consideration meant that front wheel drive models had a floor that was 100mm below that found on rear wheel drive models. For firms moving heavy loads, this made for easier loading and unloading, whilst at the same time it offered a greater load space and more interior height for those carrying lighter, more bulkier goods.

Their outstanding manoeuvrability made these front wheel drive models ideal vehicles for multi-drop delivery applications. Yet, the traditional rear wheel drive options were still offered for those who required a heavier payload and did not need a low floor loading height. These users included the building and allied trades, where the Transit had long been a number one choice, as they were the ideal choice for towing trailers.

By the new century, a very wide range of efficient engines were available including the recently introduced 2.0- and 2.4-litre Duratorq TD diesel engines. The 2.4-litre Duratorq TDCi having the six-speed Duroshift EST automated shift manual transmission. Also available were the 2.3-litre petrol engine and the more economical 2.3-litre petrol/LPG Bi-fuel. As LPG retailed at approximately half the cost of petrol. it made Transit models fitted with this engine a very practical proposition from an economic point of view. Service intervals for these models were the same as the conventional petrol engine models (12,500-miles or 12 months), while Transits that were equipped with diesel engines had servicing intervals at 15,000-miles. Transmission options on all models (except the six-speed 2.4-litre Duratorq TDCi) were either the five-speed manual gearbox or the Durashift EST Automated shift manual transmission. Warranty for the Transit models remained unchanged at three-years or 100,000 miles.

Top Right: *On display at the 2005 Commercial Motor Show is an example of the Ford Transit tipper, which was fitted with the new 2.4 TDCi 16V Duratorq diesel engine and the six-speed transmission.* Trans-Pennine Archive

Middle Right: *The extremely impressive 2.4 TDCi 16V Duratorq engine, the most powerful Transit diesel engine at the time. With a class-leading torque of 375Nm at 2000rpm, common rail fuel injection, variable geometry turbo charger, dual mass flywheel and "Hydro-mount" engine mounts were among its contributions to modern engineering standards.* Trans-Pennine Archive

Bottom Right: *Again seen at the 2005 Commercial Motor Show, this crew-cab van is based on the short-wheelbase model. This illustration serves to show the extent of Ford's commitment to safety and comfort as the commodious interior clearly shows that it is on a par with modern car-like standards, allowing a gang of workmen to arrive at their destination in un-fatigued state, which is quite unlike the position found when travelling in the older models.* Trans-

Above: *This illustration here shows one of the* Hallmark *models, which were introduced during the year 2005 to mark the celebration of the Transit's 40th anniversary. The models promoted were the Hallmark, Silver Blue, and the LX Plus.*

The new Transits were styled with near vertical sides, with this minimum taper they offered maximum load-space. Even the smallest van model was capable of carrying a standard 8' x 4' sheet of board either vertically or horizontally.

Optional features to the range were extensive. including a full range of bulkhead applications. For example a full width unglazed bulkhead could be specified and when fitted into a van with unglazed rear doors, it offered an exceptionally secure load-space as there was no way anybody could tell if a van was loaded or full, or if it carried a valuable load.

Another option was the fitting of a vertical half-width mesh bulkhead, which would help to protect the driver from any shifting loads that were carried. On the issue of load security, tie-downs were also offered across the van range to keep carried cargo safely secured to the load floor, or side cargo storage rails.

The customer even had a choice of single or twin side loading doors which were a boon for local delivery work in congested city streets. Other options included a towbar with electrical kit, power-operated and heated exterior mirrors, power-operated cab windows and front cab air conditioning.

A wide range of roof transportation systems were also on offer including roof rack crossbars and ladder-holders. To aid roof-loading, a rear ladder could be safely and securely fitted to the rear of the van, yet this still left the full access and loading to the internal area capacity completely un-hindered.

The Transit family had been surprisingly expanded in 2002 when Ford introduced a Transit model to the sub-one ton market. These compact vans, the Transit Connect and Tourneo Connect vans, were built on a dedicated platform to the same exacting standards of the conventional Transit range. Yet, as a more compact vehicle, they offered more fuel economy and lower insurance. This was ideal for the smaller business user, who also had a choice of different equipment levels. On the short-wheelbase models the basic model or the L and LX vans were built to an overall length of 4,278mm, whilst the long-wheelbase models at 4,525mm long were offered in L and LX specification. A choice of four engines were also offered, all of 1.8-litre capacity; two diesel, one petrol and one petrol/LPG.

Extensive safety features were also incorporated into these models. The front of the van's structure incorporated a 'boron high-strength steel cross-member' in front of which was a steel bumper with a soft plastic shell and foam energy absorber. An additional safety measure was the optional passenger airbag, and front seat side airbag in the event of a side impact collision. Internally, as with the full size Transit, there were several options to the bulkhead. The Connect was also fitted with fold flat passenger seat for carrying extra long loads.

The load floor area could be protected by the use of an easy-cleaned floor liner, and this was actually a standard fitting on the LX models. The cabin area had an almost car-like feel and incorporated such features as a four-way adjustable steering column. Four-way adjustable driver's seat and steering column mounted audio controls came as standard, whilst a wide range of other options were available.

Top Right: *It did not come as too much of a surprise when Ford announced the Connect as the Transit was steadily moving into the higher medium commercial market and they really needed something in between the Escort based commercials and the Transit. To redress this a new model range was introduced in the sub-one tonne market for users requiring a smaller commercial vehicle.* Trans-Pennine Archive

Bottom Right: *The Transit Connect models were built on a unique dedicated platform. Note will be made in this view of the horizontal body pressings, which in addition to their decorative appearance were intended as an aid to passenger safety in the event of side impact collision. This view, taken (like that above) at the 2005 Commercial Motor Show clearly illustrates the easy loading offered by these vehicles.*

Just as this book was going to press, Ford UK released details of its upgraded Transit (pictured above), with new front-end styling. These were accompanied by other exterior detail changes and less obvious, but nevertheless improved suspension and steering. The 2006 models also had a re-designed interior, fascia-mounted gear lever and waterproof re-charging key, which Ford believes is a sector first. The new models also include new safety and security features including seven new Euro 4 emissions-compliant engines.

"Transit led the market once again in 2005 with 54,300 sales, outselling the nearest rivals by more than three-to-one," said Gary Whittam, Commercial Vehicles Director, for Ford of Britain. One again, customer needs were the driving force behind the improvements in the new Transit and this is the secret of its continuing success.

Changes to the suspension have cut noise, vibration and harshness by around 20%. The new Transit range will offer six Duratorq TDCi-branded diesel engines and one LPG-compatible petrol engine. The diesels, the first commercial vehicle units developed as part of the partnership between Ford and PSA Peugeot Citroen, include new 2.2-litre and 2.4-litre variants matched to either five-speed or six-speed 'Durashift' manual transmissions.

ACKNOWLEDGEMENTS

I would sincerely like to thank David Hill and Anne-Marie Chatterton of the Ford Motor Company and David Heywood; for without their very generous and unfailing help, this tribute to the Ford Transit could not have been achieved.